MW01104844

Eyes on the Sky

Earth

by David M. Haugen

KidHaven Press, an imprint of Gale Group, Inc.
P.O. Box 289009, San Diego, CA 92198-9009

Library of Congress Cataloging-in-Publication Data

Haugen, David M., 1969–
  Earth/by David Haugen.
    p. cm.—(Eyes on the Sky)
  Included bibliographical references.
  ISBN 0-7377-0938-3 (hardback : alk. paper)
  1. Earth—Juvenile literature. [1. Earth.] I. Title. II. Series.
  QB634.4 .H38 2002
  525—dc21

  2001002182

Copyright 2002 by KidHaven Press, an imprint of Gale
Group, Inc., P.O. Box 289009, San Diego, CA 92198-9009

Table of Contents

1
The Livable Planet

When viewed from space, the planet Earth may not seem very special. The blue-and-white swirled planet has no distinctive rings like Saturn, and it is far less impressive than gigantic Jupiter. Within the **solar system**—the name given to the sun and the nine planets that circle around it—Earth is just a medium-sized world, a trait it shares with its closest neighbors. Like all planets, Earth is round, and like the other three planets closest to the sun, it has a hard, rocky surface surrounded by an atmosphere of gases. Nothing would seem to suggest that Earth is special in any way, and yet it is. Unlike the other planets in the solar system, Earth is the only one known to support life. This is what makes the planet unique.

In the Right Place

Earth's unique ability to support life is a result of its place in the solar system. All of the planets in the solar system are arranged at different distances from the sun. Earth is 93 million miles away from the sun and is third in the planetary lineup. This position makes life on Earth possible. How warm a planet is depends on how far away from the sun the planet is. At its distance, Earth receives just the right amount of heat to ensure that one vital ingredient for life can exist on the planet. That vital ingredient is water.

Water is needed to support both plants and animals on Earth. If Earth were much closer to the sun, the heat from the sun would be greater and the water in the oceans and rivers would boil away. Venus, the second planet from the sun, has a dry, hot landscape with no water and no life. On the other hand, if Earth were any farther away from the sun, it would be a much colder place and the water in the oceans and rivers would freeze. Mars, the fourth planet from the sun, is very cold and its water is locked up in polar ice caps. Although life may once have existed on Mars, scientists can find no evidence of life there today.

The Benefits of Sunlight

Water is only one element required for life on the planet; the sun's energy is another. The sun produces a great deal of energy that it sends out in the form of heat and light. On Earth, plants use the sun's light energy to make food. The leaves of plants absorb **carbon dioxide**—a common gas that is expelled in the breath of animals. The leaves also gather sunlight, and that energy powers a process called **photosynthesis**. During photosynthesis, plants turn the carbon dioxide gas into simple sugars. These simple sugars are the basic building blocks of all life.

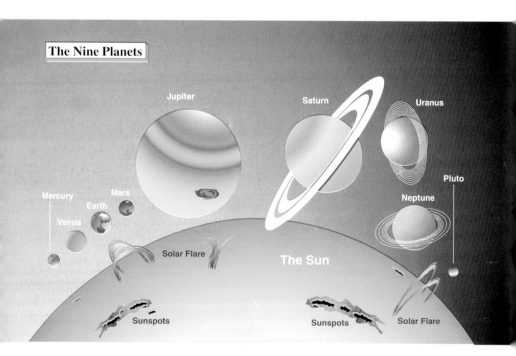

The Nine Planets

Jupiter

Saturn

Uranus

Pluto

Mercury

Mars

Neptune

Earth

Venus

Solar Flare

The Sun

Sunspots

Sunspots

Solar Flare

Life on Earth requires sun and water.

Animals either feed on the plants directly or eat other animals that have fed on the plants. The energy in the simple sugars passes from plants to animals to people. Another beneficial by-product of photosynthesis is **oxygen**. This gas is released from the carbon dioxide as it is turned into sugar. Oxygen is what animals breathe, and it is necessary for all animal life on the planet.

Since light is so important to life on the planet, it is fortunate that all parts of Earth are touched by sunlight at some time. This is because Earth rotates as it moves around, or **orbits**, the sun. It takes twenty-four hours for Earth to spin once on its axis, the imaginary pole on which the planet revolves. During this time, half of the world receives daytime sunlight while the other half is cloaked in the darkness of nighttime. While the sun shines on part of Earth, the plants on that half receive the energy needed to make food and oxygen.

The Warmth of the Sun

The sun's heat plays as important a role in plant and animal life on Earth as does the light energy it provides. The world is not uniformly hot or cold. Some days it is cold and snowy, while other days it is hot and humid. This change in temperature and climate occurs regularly over a year's time and gives rise to the seasons. Both Earth's lower half, or Southern Hemisphere, and the upper half, or Northern Hemisphere, experience seasonal changes. This is because Earth does not revolve on an axis that is straight up and down. Instead, Earth's axis is tilted so that as the planet makes its 365-day orbit around the sun, one hemisphere will be closer to the sun than the other hemisphere for part of the year. The hemisphere that is closer to the sun

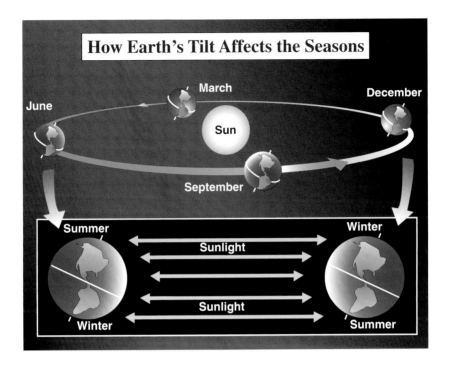

How Earth's Tilt Affects the Seasons

March

June

December

Sun

September

Summer

Winter

Sunlight

Sunlight

Winter

Summer

experiences warm summer weather while the one that is tilted away has cooler winter temperatures. Only the parts of the world lying along the **equator**, or the planet's middle section, have fairly consistent warm weather because they are nearly the same distance away from the sun year-round.

Warm temperatures help plants grow and thrive. This increases their production of food and oxygen. During winter months in very cold climates, plants lie dormant, or inactive. Many trees and bushes, for example, shed their leaves in winter months. Without leaves they cannot make new food. Only when the spring season comes around and warm weather reappears do these plants sprout new leaves and start the photosynthesis process again.

A Long Winter Sleep

Some animals are also dormant during the winter months. In the Northern Hemisphere, many species of bears, for example, spend the winters in hibernation, a state of complete rest in which they do not move in order to conserve energy. In the frigid months of winter, food is often scarce and some animals such as bears would use up their energy quickly looking for what little prey remained. As the wildlife returns in springtime, the hibernating animals are roused to forage once again for the food—either plant or animal—that thrives in the warmer temperatures.

The Place to Study Life

Earth's distance from the sun coupled with the amount of light and heat it receives allow life to thrive on the planet. No other planet in the solar system has such ideal conditions. Scientists are not sure whether other planets may have some form of life or the remnants of past life on them, but so far no space missions have ever found traces of life on the planets they have visited. And although studying other planets can help reveal more about where life can and cannot exist, many scientists know that the best subject of investigation is their own planet, Earth.

2
Earth's Atmosphere

Surrounding the entire planet Earth is an atmosphere of gases commonly called air. Earth is not the only planet to have an atmosphere, but it is the only one composed of breathable air.

The air on Earth contains oxygen, carbon dioxide, and other gases. Oxygen is what people and animals inhale while breathing, so this gas is another favorable element—like the sun's energy and the presence of water—that helps sustain life on the planet.

The Upper Atmosphere

Earth's atmosphere extends for approximately three hundred miles from the planet's surface. It is divided into four separate layers,

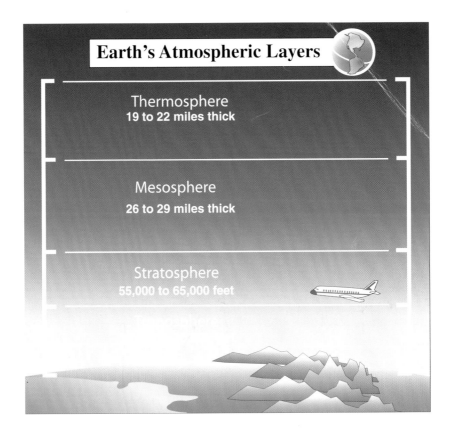

Earth's Atmospheric Layers

Thermosphere
19 to 22 miles thick

Mesosphere
26 to 29 miles thick

Stratosphere
55,000 to 65,000 feet

each one different from the next. The highest layer, called the thermosphere, begins fifty miles from Earth's surface and extends toward space. Very little air exists in this highest layer since **radiation** from the sun changes the gas particles that end up here.

The layer below the thermosphere is called the mesosphere. This layer occupies the region between thirty and fifty miles from the planet's surface. The mesosphere is home to some high-level clouds that are thought to be made of ice crystals. Called noctilucent, these unusual clouds are only visible on summer nights.

The layer extending from about six miles to thirty miles from Earth is called the stratosphere. Some clouds, called nacreous clouds, form here and are visible when the sun sits just below the horizon. Temperatures in the upper stratosphere are very cold, more than 70 degrees Fahrenheit below zero.

The Ozone Layer

Within the lowest levels of the stratosphere is a thin layer of gas called ozone. Ozone is a form of oxygen, and the ozone layer is important for the planet's survival. The ozone layer reflects a lot of the sun's harmful radiation back into space. If large amounts of the sun's radiation reached Earth, it would damage or kill living creatures.

Scientists are aware of how important the ozone layer is to the planet. They worry that the ozone layer is being destroyed by chemicals called **chlorofluorocarbons**, or CFCs. These chemicals are used in many man-made devices from aerosol sprays to refrigerator coolants. CFCs were considered very beneficial when they were introduced in the 1920s because they aren't poisonous when sprayed and they last a long time in cooling ma-

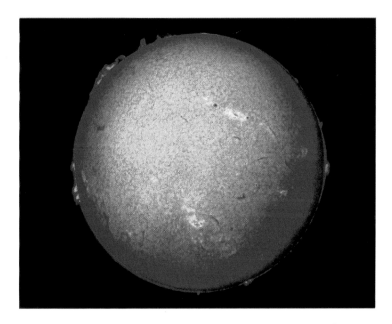

The sun. The ozone layer protects Earth from the sun's harmful radiation.

chines like refrigerators and air conditioners. It wasn't until the 1970s that scientists realized CFCs were drifting up into the stratosphere and causing a thinning of the ozone layer. Once the danger of CFCs was brought to the attention of the world, most nations agreed to limit their use. Still, substitutes have been difficult to find, and CFCs remain part of many household products.

Wind and Weather

Below the ozone layer and the lower reaches of the stratosphere is the last level of Earth's atmosphere. Called the troposphere, this layer of the atmosphere is where the planet's weather occurs. Weather and climate are influenced by the movement of air in the troposphere. Because the regions near Earth's equator receive the most heat from the sun all year long, the air there is warmer than in other areas of the globe. Colder air from the Northern and Southern Hemispheres rushes in to fill the space left empty by the rising warm air. When this air heats up, it also rises and pushes the warm air above it toward the Northern and Southern Hemispheres. This process is repeated over and over again and accounts for the movement of winds on the planet.

The Formation of Clouds

Besides carrying warmth to many parts of the world, the winds also carry water. As the sun heats the air in the tropical areas near the equator, it also heats the oceans below. The water in these oceans evaporates as steam into the warm air. As the steam rises into the atmosphere, it cools back into water droplets. Together millions of these water droplets form clouds in the troposphere. The clouds are pushed northward and southward by the movement of air.

The water in the clouds becomes cooler as the clouds move away from the equator.

The wind carries water to many parts of the world.

When the atmospheric temperature is cold enough, the droplets freeze and fall as icy flakes. In most seasons, the warm weather causes the flakes to melt as they drop, and the water falls as rain. In winter, though, cold weather prevents the icy flakes from melting and they fall as sleet or snow. Rain and snow are very important to life since they bring water to the interior of the land masses on Earth. Some of this water ends up in lakes and rivers and becomes drinking water for people and animals. The rest sinks into the ground, where it is soaked up by the roots of plants, helping them to grow.

Storms

In many rain clouds the droplets of water often collide as they travel through the air. The striking of one droplet against another causes the droplets to become electrically charged. The building electric charge in the cloud sometimes lashes out in the form of lightning. As the lightning passes through the air, it heats it up until

Lightning is formed by electrical charges in clouds.

A picture of a hurricane taken from outer space.

some of the superheated air molecules explode. The sound of this explosion is thunder.

Thunder and lightning often signal the arrival of a storm. Rainstorms are common throughout the world, and if their accompanying winds are not too strong, then they are generally good for the land and its inhabitants. However, if the winds in storms grow stronger and travel at much higher speeds, storms can become dangerous. Hurricanes are storms that form over warm oceans. Their winds can reach up to 125 miles per hour, about four times as forceful as a strong breeze. Gathering wind and water as they travel, these storms can cause great damage if they reach land. Coastal areas that experience hurricanes are usually drenched with rain, which can ruin crops and cause flooding. Trees can be uprooted and even heavier objects like houses can be crushed by the fierce winds. Luckily, weather experts, or meteorologists, can track hurricanes when they are still out at sea, giving inhabitants of coastal areas plenty of time to safeguard themselves and their belongings before the storm reaches land.

Similar to hurricanes, tornadoes are strong windstorms that cause damage to anything in their path. Unlike hurricanes, however, tornadoes strike inland and their winds can travel

Tornadoes are funnel-shaped windstorms.

faster than two hundred miles per hour. They also typically arise without warning, although meteorologists can generally predict the kinds of weather that are favorable to the creation of tornadoes. Once a tornado forms, the huge funnel-shaped, dark cloud of windswept dust and debris touches ground and then travels in a straight line until the wind strength dies. This path may extend for several miles, and everything in the tornado's way may be lifted into the air and carried for some distance before it is flung back to the ground.

Benefiting Life

Hurricanes and tornadoes show one extreme of Earth's weather. Most weather phenomena are not so destructive. Milder winds and rains benefit life on Earth by bringing warm temperatures and water to different parts of the world. Only through this process can plant and animal life exist far inland from the oceans of the planet. Earth's weather patterns, then, ensure that life can spread out across the landscape, inhabiting nearly every corner of the planet.

3
A Landscape in Motion

Anyone looking at images of the planet taken from space is bound to recognize the big, dark patches of oceans and the hard-edged shape of the continents. These features of Earth's landscape are familiar to many because they appear in the same arrangement from photo to photo. North America rests just above South America, connected by the strand of countries between Mexico and Colombia. The huge land mass that makes up the continents of Europe and Asia lies just across the Atlantic Ocean from North America. The pattern of these continents and oceans—and the others spread across the planet—remains the same whether seen in a satellite image or on a classroom globe.

Earth as seen from space.

What these images of the planet don't reveal, however, is that the landscape is actually moving. Although the oceans and continents—seen from far above the planet—appear to be static and unchanging, the landscape below is very much in motion. In fact, Earth's surface features have been changing ever since the planet was born over 4.5 billion years ago.

The Rolling Waters

Perhaps the most obvious movement notice-able on the planet is that of its oceans and in-land waterways, such as rivers and streams. Water covers about 70 percent of the planet, and most of it is in constant motion. The huge oceans of the world hold over 97 percent of the water on Earth. The water within them is called salt water because of the large amounts of salt that is dissolved in it. Winds drive the salt water near the surface of the oceans, and cur-rents move the salt water in the depths below. Although it is out in space, Earth's moon also

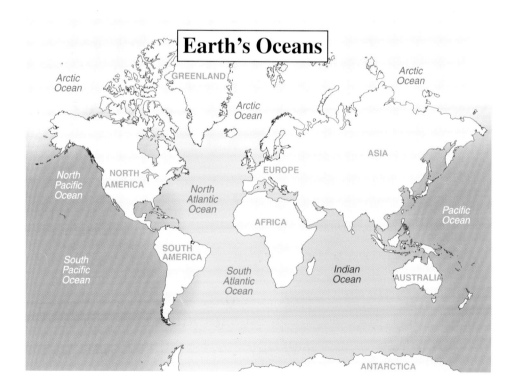

Earth's Oceans

The gravitational pull of the moon (below) on the earth (above) causes tides.

affects the movement of the oceans by pulling on them with its **gravity**. The gravitational pull of the moon causes the tides. The tides rise and fall according to the position of the moon in relation to the planet. Together, winds, under-water currents, and tides push and pull the ocean's salt water around the globe.

A Landscape in Motion   25

Salt water is not the type of water that people drink. Drinking water comes from the world's freshwater sources, such as lakes and rivers. Freshwater does not contain the large amounts of salt that could harm any person who drank salt water.

Freshwater Sources

Freshwater comes from rain and snow, water from the sea that has been evaporated by the sun's heat and left its salt behind. When carried inland by clouds, the rain or snow falls to Earth and deposits in the inland rivers and lakes. Some snow falls in the high mountains, where the cooler temperatures keep it frozen longer. Eventually, however, the mountain snow packs melt, and the water rolls down into rivers that start in these high elevations.

Most of the planet's rivers start in the snow-topped mountains. Earth's gravity then pulls the water down to lower elevations. Sometimes the rivers end up in lakes, where the water will evaporate into the air. The world's largest rivers, however, typically empty into the sea, having reached the lowest elevation along their paths. There, at the mouth of each river that reaches the sea, the freshwater mingles with salt water and the oceans are replenished. As the sun heats up

Freshwater rivers mingle with saltwater when they flow into the ocean.

the oceans and causes more water to evaporate, the process begins again.

Drifting Continents

Although it is easy to think of Earth's oceans and rivers in constant motion, it is more difficult to imagine that the land is also moving. Of course, the land does not travel fast like the water in a rushing river, but even the huge continents shift their positions every year—even if only by a few inches. The land moves because Earth's crust—its outer shell of rock—is not solid. Forces deep within the planet have broken the crust into several huge pieces called plates. These plates drift on the molten bed of rock that lies just below the planet's crust. Over time they may drift a long way.

Some scientists believe that millions of years ago the arrangement of the continents may have been very different than the way they appear now. These scientists think that the continents may all have been joined in one land mass and that over Earth's history they drifted to their current positions. Millions of years into the future, then, the continents may have drifted to new positions, making their arrangement unfamiliar to anyone looking at today's world maps.

Creating Mountains

As Earth's plates move, they separate from some neighboring plates and collide with others. Where the plates crash, the land is forced upward and mountains form. The Rocky Mountains in North America, the Andes in South America, and the Himalayas of Asia are all evidence of places where plates have pushed up against each other. The Himalayas are the tallest mountains in the world, and they rest where two plates are still colliding.

The movement of Earth's plates formed the Himalayas.

Every year the forces of the collision push rock upward and add a fraction of an inch to the height of the Himalayas, meaning these mountains are still growing.

Volcanoes

Sometimes when plates crash head-on, they don't both push upward. Often, one plate may slide underneath the other. When this happens, the edge of the plate that slides downward is melted by the heat under the planet's crust. If there are any cracks between the two plates, this molten rock can escape to

A picture of Mount Saint Helens after its 1980 eruption.

the surface. The molten rock is pressed upward out of the land and forms a volcano. Volcanoes erupt, spewing lava (molten rock), ash,
steam, and smoke into the air. The land for
miles around the volcano can be scorched by
the high temperatures. When Mount Saint
Helens erupted in Washington State in 1980,
everything within eighteen miles of the volcano was burned by either hot ash or bursts
of hot gases. Huge forests were charred black
by the tremendous heat. Lava that spreads

out from volcanic eruptions also covers over the surrounding landscape. Eventually when this lava cools, it will be the new ground on which new plants and trees will grow.

Not all volcanoes occur on land. Some of the strongest erupt underwater. When this happens, the lava rock will cool faster as it mixes with the water. Sometimes the lava will cool so quickly that it piles up faster than it can spread out. Eventually the rock will break the surface of the water and form an island. Many islands in the Pacific Ocean have been formed this way. The Hawaiian Islands, for example, are the visible tops of volcanoes that extend down into the ocean. These volcanoes erupted 40 million years ago, and over time vegetation and wildlife covered the islands, turning them into the lush, tropical paradises they are today.

Earthquakes

Volcanic eruptions are often predictable. Scientists monitor volcanoes, and the information they gather can help save the lives of anyone living near a "hot spot," or area of volcanic activity. When Mount Saint Helens erupted, only a few people lost their lives because scientists had warned against the coming danger and most people had left the area.

In 1994, the Northridge earthquake in California destroyed buildings such as this parking garage.

Earthquakes, which also result from movement of the land, are more difficult to predict. Scientists know where earthquakes are likely to happen, but it is difficult to determine exactly when they will strike.

Deep inside the planet, layers of molten rock shift position frequently. The outer crust of Earth, however, is solid and resists the pull of the molten rock below. Eventually, the strain builds up and the rocks of the crust give way and break apart. This energy released from the built-up stress is sent out as shock waves from the center of the earthquake. The shock waves rumble through the planet and violently shake the ground. Anything that is not secure can be overturned or knocked down. Buildings and bridges may crumble or collapse as they did during the 1994 Northridge earthquake that struck a section of Los Angeles. This moderate earthquake damaged more than twelve thousand buildings and several major freeways as it shook the crowded suburb.

Despite the damage earthquakes can do to buildings and property, the violent shaking is not the biggest cause of injury or death. Instead, earthquakes often set off rock or mud slides that bury everything in their path. Also, the jarring of the ground may rupture gas and power lines in major cities, and the resulting fires are more likely to claim lives than the collapse of buildings. Thankfully, many earthquakes occur so far underground that the people living above feel only a slight trembling that passes in a matter of seconds.

Volcanoes and earthquakes are some of the more forceful reminders that the planet's surface is still in a process of change. Just as the plants and animals on Earth grow and change, so too does the entire planet. The constant movement of the land and the waters show that the planet is still living and still capable of supporting the many varieties of life on its surface.

4

Where to Find Life on Earth

Although Earth offers a lot of space for life to flourish, not all parts of the globe are teeming with plants and animals. If there were a satellite image that showed where all life-forms were on the planet, it would reveal that plants and animals tend to group together in certain regions of the world. Life thrives in these places because they offer more favorable living conditions than can be found on other parts of the planet. The abundance of food and water, along with a warm, comfortable climate, attract plants, animals, and people to these thriving areas. Regions of the world that have fewer favorable necessities can only maintain smaller pockets of life.

Seas and Wetlands

The huge oceans that cover Earth hold many kinds of life. All sorts of fish and mammals swim through the salt water or crawl along the ocean floors. Plants, such as seaweed, also grow at the bottom of the ocean, while microscopic plant life called plankton floats on the surface. Plankton is important to life because, like all green plants, it turns carbon dioxide into oxygen. Huge floating "fields" of plankton are one of Earth's main suppliers of

Plankton live along the shores of the continents.

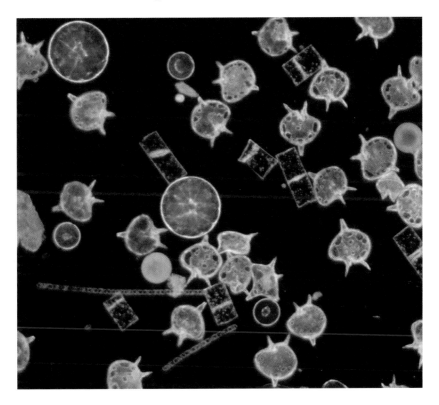

this precious, breathable gas. Plankton is also important because it is the food source for many small fish. Since small fish are eaten by bigger fish, which in turn are preyed upon by larger marine life, plankton is the origin of the ocean's food chain.

Despite the vast area the world's oceans cover, most of the plankton masses are along the shores of the continents. In fact, marine plants and animals of all kinds seem to cling to the edges of the land. This is because the shores are where rivers and oceans meet. The river waters bring rich nutrients from inland to the plankton waiting offshore. Since the plankton grows large here, the fish that feed off it are also most abundant along the coasts.

Marshy Wetlands

In many regions where rivers flow into the ocean, the landscape is covered in marshes and wetlands. These areas are home not only to fish and other sea creatures, but also to birds and animals that are at home both on the land and in the water. Alligators, for example, glide through the wetlands around the southern coast of the United States. Many species of shorebirds and turtles also make their home in this marshy land, while gentle manatees swim in the waters offshore. The

Lightning flashes over a wetland area.

great variety of life along coastal wetlands re-
veals that they are favorite habitats for sea life
as well as plants and animals from the land.

Harsh Landscapes

Similar to life in the sea, the many types of
plants and animals that live on the land clus-
ter around certain areas of the globe. Many
such areas exist on Earth; plants and animals
can live in almost every region of the globe. In
some places, however, harsh conditions limit
plant and animal life. In frozen Antarctica, for

example, the land is barren and snow covered. Without protection from the cold and without a variety of plants or animals to eat, most creatures would perish. Some have adapted to this unfriently landscape, however. Penguins, for example, have little trouble existing in this climate. They have bodies that resist the cold temperatures, and they feed on the fish that live along the shore.

In deserts, such as the Sahara of Africa or the Gobi of Asia, the harsh climate and lack of water create a similarly unfriendly environment. Desert plants and animals have the ability to conserve the water they do find, however. In the deserts of the American Southwest and Mexico, for example, cactus grows with very little water, and several species of this plant carry sharp needles to protect themselves from scavenging animals who want the precious water they do carry. Such regions as deserts and polar lands, then, are home to some of Earth's life-forms, but much less than can be found in parts of the world that enjoy milder climates.

The Temperate Zones

Most of the planet's wildlife lives where temperatures are warm and rain is plentiful. Some of these regions are called temperate

A dust storm whips through the Sahara Desert.

zones because they have mild climates for most of the year. Temperate zones exist north and south of the equator and run through most of the world's continents. Grasslands and forests are common in these regions, giving homes to many types of birds and mammals as well as trees, shrubs, and grasses.

Most people also live in the temperate regions. They prefer to live in climates where warm temperatures and rain are common at least during part of the year. This provides a comfortable living environment and ensures that food crops will get sun and water to grow.

The presence of food and water determine where people choose to live. Like the preference of sea creatures to live close to shore, most people live near rivers, lakes, and oceans (especially where rivers drain). The freshwater is needed to drink, but it also provides nutrients to the surrounding land, making good soil to grow food. Large bodies of water like lakes and oceans also have a cooling effect on local temperatures, keeping the climate mild and enjoyable year-round.

The Tropical Rain Forests

Although fewer people live in the forested regions around the equator than in other areas, the greatest variety of life is found there. Temperatures are hot and rain falls throughout the year. This climate creates lush tropical rain forests that are home to more plant and animal species than anywhere else in the world. There are so many species of insects, birds, reptiles, and plants that some have yet to be named.

The large amount of plant life in the rain forests of the world is another major supplier of the planet's oxygen. The exotic plants are also sources of medicines used worldwide. Despite these important functions, many of the world's rain forests are being cut down. The nations

Tropical rain forests are found near the equator.

where rain forests exist are often poor, and the land is being cleared to make room for farms to help feed the growing populations. Unfortunately, the soil of rain forest regions is not hardy enough to support crops for long, and farmers simply clear more forest land when their farmland is drained of its nutrients.

Many people in countries around the world are speaking out against the destruction of the rain forests. They believe there is a better way to maintain the valuable forest regions and provide for the increasing number of people on the planet. So far, however, the need for land and food has outweighed the desire to conserve the rain forests and land is still being cleared.

The Balance

The plight of the rain forests is just one example of the effects a growing number of people are having upon the planet. As the world's population increases, so does the need for more land, food, and water. The people spread out and turn wilderness into farmlands and cities. These changes can cause damage to the environment. The growth in population means an increase in pollution, and the claiming of wilderness for human use may cause the extinction of animal and plant species that inhabit that land.

The relationship between people and the environment is delicate. Only humans have the ability to care for the planet by managing their needs and maintaining a healthy environment at the same time. Striking the balance will ensure that Earth, the uniquely livable planet, continues to support all kinds of life for many years to come.

Glossary

carbon dioxide: A gas that is not breathable to humans. Carbon dioxide that people and other animals breathe out is taken in by plants, which, in turn, convert the gas into breathable oxygen.

chlorofluorocarbons (CFCs): Man-made chemicals used in many products such as aerosol sprays and the coolant systems of refrigerators and air conditioners. CFCs released into the air eventually travel up to the stratosphere. There, the chlorine gas is released from the CFCs and eats away at the protective ozone layer.

equator: An imaginary line that circles the middle of Earth, separating the Northern Hemisphere from the Southern Hemisphere.

gravity: The force of attraction. Gravity on Earth draws all matter to the surface of the planet.

orbit: The path of one heavenly body revolving around another. The revolving body is held in orbit partly by the gravity of the central body. This helps explain why an orbiting body continues to revolve around the central body instead of flying off into space.

oxygen: One of the breathable gases that is common in air.

photosynthesis: A process in green plants that turns carbon dioxide into simple sugars. The by-product of photosynthesis is oxygen, which plants release into the air.

radiation: Heat or light energy common in the universe. The sun sends radiation to Earth in the form of light and heat. Since too much radiation can damage living things, Earth has many protective barriers—such as the ozone layer—that repel much of the sun's radiation, allowing only a small amount to reach the surface of the planet.

solar system: The sun and the collection of planets, moons, and other smaller planetoid objects (such as asteroids) that revolve around it. Earth is the third planet from the sun.

For Further
Exploration

Books

Neil Curtis and Michael Allaby, *Visual Fact-finder: Planet Earth*. New York: Kingfisher, 1993. An excellent resource on Earth. Sections focus on a single topic (such as the atmosphere, volcanoes, and plate tectonics), allowing for a fair amount of detail on each. Good illustrations help explain more complex ideas.

Jill Hamilton, ed., *Nature Encyclopedia*, New York: DK Publishing, 1998. A large volume on the variety of plant and animal life on Earth. This encyclopedia not only catalogs various life-forms, but also has sections on the biology of some animals and the internal structure of plants. Pictures and illustrations fill the book, making it very attractive and accessible.

Sally Ride and Tam O'Shaughnessy, *The Third Planet: Exploring Earth from Space*. New York: Crown Publishers, 1994. A good, easy-to-follow overview of Earth written by the astronaut Sally Ride. Ride blends her own experiences into the text, keeping readers interested in the many topics she covers.

Websites

NASA Kids. (http://kids.msfc.nasa.gov) This is the National Aeronautics and Space Administration's website designed especially for kids. There is very basic information here on the planets and many fun projects to try. The site is updated regularly with reports on the best times to view astronomical events as well as upcoming NASA projects.

Index